Sioux

F.A. BIRD

CONTENT CONSULTANT: CHARMAINE WHITE FACE

Checkerboard Library

An Imprint of Abdo Publishing
abdobooks.com

ABDOBOOKS.COM

Published by Abdo Publishing, a division of ABDO, PO Box 398166, Minneapolis, Minnesota 55439. Copyright © 2022 by Abdo Consulting Group, Inc. International copyrights reserved in all countries. No part of this book may be reproduced in any form without written permission from the publisher. Checkerboard Library™ is a trademark and logo of Abdo Publishing.

Printed in the United States of America, North Mankato, Minnesota
102021
012022

THIS BOOK CONTAINS RECYCLED MATERIALS

Design and Production: Mighty Media, Inc.
Editor: Liz Salzmann
Cover Photograph: Jeff Wallager/iStockphoto
Interior Photographs: Ad_hominem/Shutterstock Images, p. 7; CharlotteMB/iStockphoto, p. 29; David F. Barry/Wikimedia Commons, p. 27; GPA Photo Archive/Flickr, p. 19; Jess Kraft/Shutterstock Images, p. 5; joeygil/iStockphoto, p. 15; Joseph Sohm/Shutterstock Images, p. 25; Karla Caspari/Shutterstock Images, p. 13; Library of Congress, p. 23; National Museum of the American Indian, Smithsonian Institution (N53814), p. 17; nyker/Shutterstock Images, p. 9; Ronnie Howard/Shutterstock Images, p. 21; Tom Reichner/Shutterstock Images, p. 11

Library of Congress Control Number: 2021942979

Publisher's Cataloging-in-Publication Data
Names: Bird, F.A., author.
Title: Sioux / by F.A. Bird
Description: Minneapolis, Minnesota : Abdo Publishing, 2022 | Series: Native American nations | Includes online resources and index.
Identifiers: ISBN 9781532197239 (lib. bdg.) | ISBN 9781098219369 (ebook)
Subjects: LCSH: American Indians--Juvenile literature. | Indians of North America--Juvenile literature. | Indigenous peoples--Social life and customs--Juvenile literature. | Cultural anthropology--Juvenile literature.
Classification: DDC 973.0497--dc23

Contents

Homelands 4
Society 6
Homes 8
Food 10
Clothing 12
Crafts 14
Family 16
Children 18
Traditions 20
War 22
Contact with Europeans 24
Sitting Bull 26
The Sioux Today 28
Glossary 30
Online Resources 31
Index 32

CHAPTER 1

Homelands

The Sioux name comes from the Ojibwa word *Nadouessioux* (nay-doo-we-sue). It means "little snakes" or "lesser enemies." In the 1700s, French traders and trappers shortened this Ojibwa word to "Sioux." However, the Sioux nation call themselves *Oceti Sakowin* (oh-shet-ee shah-ko-ween), which means "Seven Council Fires."

Many Sioux creation stories say their homelands were in the Black Hills of present-day South Dakota. The Black Hills are sacred to the Sioux people. Others say the Sioux came from the woodlands of present-day northern Minnesota. By the time Europeans arrived in America, the Sioux controlled most of the **Great Plains**.

Many Sioux still live in the Black Hills of South Dakota. This region gets its name because its tree-covered hills appear black when viewed from far away.

CHAPTER 2

Society

The Sioux all speak the same language. But there are three different dialects. These are Dakota, Nakota, and Lakota. The Sioux were divided into seven subnations. Each subnation was made up of one to seven **bands**, or *ospaye* (oh-shpie-ye).

A band included several extended families called *tiospaye* (tee-oh-shpie-ye) who all had a common ancestor. When a couple got married, they lived with the woman's *tiospaye*.

Sioux leaders were older women. The leaders were chosen by the people. They were chosen because they had shown their wisdom and love for the people. Leaders did not tell others what to do. Instead, they gave suggestions and recommendations. Decisions for the entire band were made at meetings. The discussions continued until everyone agreed.

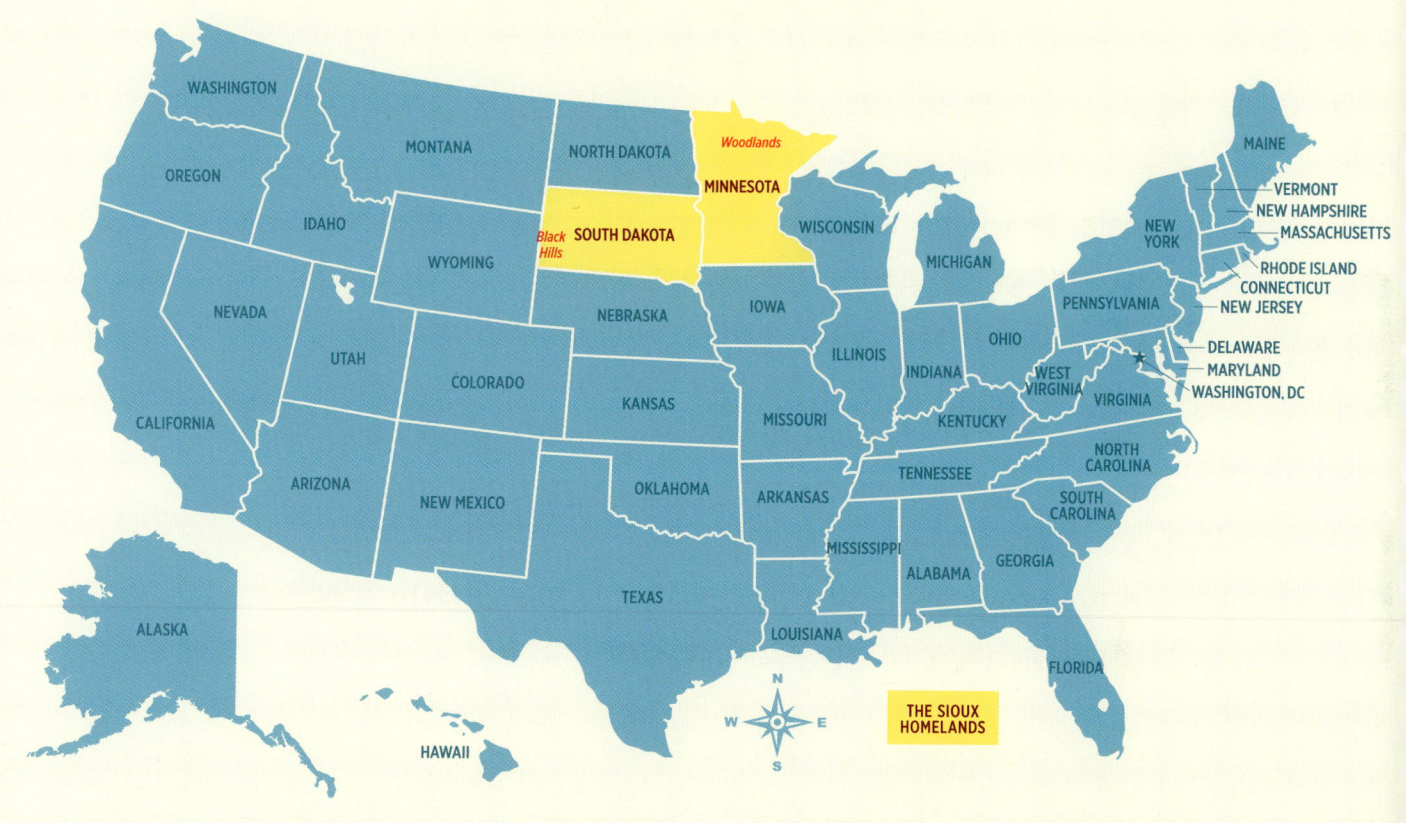

Homes

The Sioux lived in tepees. A tepee's frame is made of pine poles tied together at the top. The bottom of the poles spread out to form a large circle. The frame is wrapped with buffalo hides that are sewn together. The top of the tepee has two flaps that allow smoke to escape from a fire pit in the center of the circle.

When they traveled, the Sioux used the tepee poles to make **travois**. A travois could carry heavy loads. A dog could pull a travois weighing 30 to 50 pounds (14 to 23 km). Horses could pull much heavier travois. Horses could also carry people too old or too sick to walk.

Many Native Plains peoples used tepees.

CHAPTER 4

Food

The Sioux were hunters, gatherers, and traders. They ate rice, beans, vegetables, fruits, deer, turkey, fish, and other animals. Buffalo was the most important food. No part was wasted. Buffalo skin was used for tepee coverings, sleeping robes, floor rugs, moccasins, and other clothing. The bones and horns were used for cups, spoons, needles, and many other utensils.

Buffalo and some other meats were preserved by drying. The meat was cut into thin strips and hung on wooden drying racks. The dried meat was then stored in bags. Dried meat was light and easy to carry. It could be stored to be eaten in the winter. The Sioux also made pemmican, or *wasna* (wah-snah). This was a mixture of dried meat, dried berries, and bone marrow.

South Dakota's prairies were once home to millions of buffalo. Today, about 33,000 live in the state.

Clothing

All Sioux clothing was made from animal hides. Men wore shirts, **breechcloths**, and leggings. Men also wore hats made from animal skins. Women wore dresses and leggings. The seams and hems of dresses, leggings, and shirts often had long **fringe**. Men and women sometimes wore **sashes** around the waist or over the shoulder. All men, women, and children wore their hair in two braids.

Everyone wore moccasins made from animal hides. In the winter, the moccasins had fur inside to keep the person's feet warm. The winter moccasins were also made waterproof with oil from different plants and animals. Buffalo robes were also used as winter coats and as blankets.

A man dances in traditional clothing at a Sioux *wacipi*, or powwow, near Mankato, Minnesota.

CHAPTER 6

Crafts

The Sioux people did many activities which are now called crafts. They often painted the outsides of tepees. This was so others would know who lived there. The paints came from clay, certain rocks, and plants.

Paintings were also used to keep track of important events. These paintings were called Winter Counts. They sometimes only had one symbol per year to trigger the memory of an event.

The Sioux sometimes decorated clothes with porcupine **quills**. Doing quillwork was a winter activity and required a lot of skill, patience, and time. In the late 1800s, glass beads from the Europeans began to replace porcupine quills. Today, the Sioux still do quillwork and beadwork.

Moccasins were often decorated with beadwork designs that had special meaning.

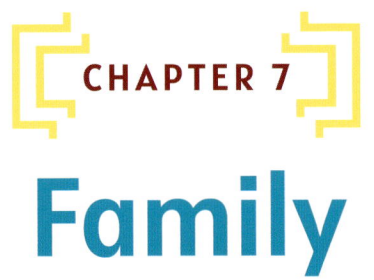

CHAPTER 7
Family

Kinship is very important to the Sioux. The Sioux believe that in addition to their human family, they have a familial relationship with the rest of creation, including Mother Earth. The Sioux believe that protecting their family and Mother Earth is their responsibility.

The Sioux believe it is important to respect themselves and others. One way the Sioux showed respect for someone was to not use their name. Instead, they referred to their relationship. For example, the oldest boy in a family was called "eldest brother" by his brothers and sisters. He was called "eldest son" by his parents, and "male cousin" by his cousins.

A Sioux family in the late 1800s

CHAPTER 8
Children

The Sioux considered children to be sacred. They believed that newborn babies came from the Spirit World. Caring for children was the responsibility of all the people. Since they usually lived surrounded by relatives, the children could play wherever they wanted. Grandparents often looked after the children.

Children were taught to be quiet as toddlers. Being quiet was necessary for the survival of all the people. Adults even used quiet voices to scold children.

When a boy turned 12, he went to live in the Men's Lodge with other unmarried men. There, he was taught the things men needed to know. Girls lived with their parents until they were married.

Lakota children prepare to dance at a powwow.

CHAPTER 9
Traditions

The Sioux have traditions going back thousands of years. They have origin stories to explain where they came from. They also have stories about the Great Flood. Grandparents taught these stories to the children. However, learning these stories was later banned by the US government. So, only a few Sioux still know them.

One story is about Sacred White Buffalo Calf Woman. Long ago in a time of great hunger, two warriors went hunting. They saw a beautiful woman with long hair. The next day, the woman appeared in the camp. She taught the people many ceremonies and gave them the Buffalo Calf Pipe. The woman promised to return once during each age and bring peace.

The woman then changed into a black buffalo. Next, she changed into a red-brown buffalo. Then, she changed into a yellow buffalo. Finally, she changed into a white buffalo and disappeared.

The Sioux consider white buffalo to be sacred. These animals are very rare. Only about one in every 10 million buffalo is born white.

War

Sioux warriors fought bravely to protect their people. In war, they carried a shield and a lance, or a bow and arrows. The weapons were made from natural material such as wood, leather, bones, and stone.

The Sioux were excellent riders. Their horses were well trained and fast. The horses allowed the men to move quickly in battle and escape danger. When the Sioux learned to handle guns, they became excellent marksmen.

Conflict was unavoidable with the coming of the Europeans and their different values and lifestyles. As more Europeans came to the Sioux homelands, all Sioux men, women, and children were taught to defend themselves and their relatives.

Sioux warrior Turning Bear wears a bone breast plate. It was a type of armor.

Contact with Europeans

In the 1600s, the Sioux met French fur traders and explorers near Lake Superior. In 1658, the first Treaty of Peace and Friendship was made between France and the Sioux. In 1804, American explorers Meriwether Lewis and William Clark met Sioux people near the Missouri River.

The French and Americans had cloth, brass kettles, wheat flour, coffee, glass beads, and guns to trade. The Sioux traded with furs, **quill** and beadwork, dried food, leather clothes, and other goods.

In 1868, the last treaty between the United States and the Sioux was signed in what is now Wyoming. The treaty said the Sioux would be able to remain in the Black Hills. However, Europeans discovered gold in the Black Hills in 1874. The Sioux were forced onto **reservations** so the Europeans could mine the gold.

Horses are still an important part of Sioux culture. Many Sioux show off their horse skills in rodeos.

CHAPTER 12
Sitting Bull

Sitting Bull was born in present-day South Dakota in 1831. As a young man, he received the name Sitting Bull for his bravery. Sitting Bull later became a respected **medicine man** and leader.

In 1876, the United States wanted to buy Sioux land. But the Sioux did not want to sell the land. The US government sent Lieutenant Colonel George Armstrong Custer and his troops to fight the Sioux. There were many bloody battles.

One of these battles was the Battle of the Little Bighorn. On June 25, 1876, Custer and his army attacked Sitting Bull's village. Sitting Bull organized the village's defense. Another Sioux leader, Crazy Horse, led the Sioux warriors to surround Custer's troops. Custer and all of his soldiers were killed.

In 1890, Sitting Bull was arrested. His neighbors and family tried to stop the arrest. This caused a fight, and Sitting Bull was killed. He is buried in Mobridge, South Dakota.

Sitting Bull

The Sioux Today

Today, there are Sioux **reservations** in North and South Dakota, Nebraska, Minnesota, and Canada. Life there is often hard. There are not enough houses or jobs, and healthcare is poor. So, many Sioux live elsewhere.

In 1929, the Sioux were made American citizens. In 1980, the **US Supreme Court** said that the Sioux should have been paid for the Black Hills. The Supreme Court offered the Sioux $102 million. But the Sioux refused the money. They said, "The sacred Black Hills are not for sale." Today, representatives go to the **United Nations** and work to have the 1868 Treaty enforced and the sacred Black Hills returned to them.

The Sioux are strong, spiritual people. They have great pride in their history and **culture**. Many try to live the traditional way of life and show respect for all things. Many also work to preserve their language, spirituality, and rights as a nation.

Powwows give members of the Sioux Nation the opportunity to celebrate their culture.

Glossary

band—a number of persons acting together; a subgroup of a tribe.

breechcloth—a piece of cloth, usually worn by men. It wraps between the legs and around the waist.

culture—the customs, arts, and tools of a nation or people at a certain time.

fringe—a border or trim made of threads or cords, either loose or tied together in small bunches.

Great Plains—a region east of the Rocky Mountains in the United States and Canada.

medicine man—a spiritual leader of a tribe or nation.

quill—a large, stiff feather or a sharp spine.

reservation—a piece of land set aside by the government for Native Americans to live on.

sash—a long, broad strip of cloth or ribbon, worn as an ornament around the waist or over one shoulder.

travois (truh-VOI)—a frame of two wooden poles tied together over the back of an animal and allowed to drag on the ground. It was used to transport loads.

United Nations—a group of nations formed in 1945. Its goals are peace, human rights, security, and social and economic development.

US Supreme Court—the highest, most powerful court in the United States.

ONLINE RESOURCES

To learn more about the Sioux, please visit **abdobooklinks.com** or scan this QR code. These links are routinely monitored and updated to provide the most current information available.

Index

animals, 8, 10, 12, 20, 22
art, 14

bands, 6
Black Hills, 4, 24, 28

Canada, 28
children, 12, 18, 20, 22
Clark, William, 24
clothes, 10, 12, 14, 24
Crazy Horse, 26
Custer, George Armstrong, 26

Dakota, 6

Europe, 4, 14, 22, 24

family, 6, 16, 18, 20
food, 10, 24
France, 4, 24

Great Plains, 4

homelands, 4, 22, 24, 26, 28
hunting, 10

Lake Superior, 24
Lakota, 6
language, 6, 28
leaders, 6, 26
Lewis, Meriwether, 24
Little Bighorn, Battle of, 26

Minnesota, 4, 28
Missouri River, 24

Nakota, 6
Nebraska, 28
North Dakota, 28

Ojibwa, 4

reservations, 24, 28

Sacred White Buffalo Calf
    Woman, 20
seasons, 10, 12, 14
Sitting Bull, 26
South Dakota, 4, 26, 28
Supreme Court, US, 28

tepees, 8, 10, 14
trading, 10, 24
treaties, 24, 28

United Nations, 28
United States, 4, 24, 26, 28

war, 22, 26
weapons, 22
Winter Counts, 14
Wyoming, 24